Are We There Yet?

Acknowledgements

Some poems first appeared in *Singer*, a pamphlet chosen by Michael Longley to be a winner in the 2008 Poetry Business Pamphlet Competition, some were first published in *Poetry Review, Poetry News, The North, MsLexia, Magma* and in *The Sheffield Anthology, Poems from the City Imagined*.

Versions of 'Spitfire', 'The Jubilee Clock' and 'Engineer, Dyeworks' were commissioned by Fleet Arts and The Derwent Valley Mills World Heritage Site and written out of interviews with ex mill workers in Derbyshire. 'Lucky' was featured in a Sheffield project, Poems on the Trams. 'Janice' was one of several poems written for a BBC Radio 4 drama by Rony Robinson and myself, Women of a Certain Age.

'Thaw' was highly commended in the 2012 National Poetry Competition; 'Are We There Yet?' was a runner up in the Mslexia Poetry Competition in 2012 and published in the magazine; 'Casualty', 'Bird' and 'Lil' were shortlisted for the Bridport Poetry Prize in 2008 and 2009; 'Thaw' and 'Dipper' were longlisted for the RSPB/Rialto Nature Competition in 2012; 'Yew and Birds' was shortlisted for the Magma Poetry Competition 2011.

I am grateful to the many poets who have helped me. Also for a Hawthornden Fellowship which enabled me to work on this collection and to write several of these poems.

Are We There Yet?
Sally Goldsmith

Best wishes
to the lovely Clive,
Sally Goldsmith

smith|doorstop

Published 2013 by
Smith/Doorstop Books
The Poetry Business
Bank Street Arts
32-40 Bank Street
Sheffield S1 2DS
www.poetrybusiness.co.uk

Copyright © Sally Goldsmith 2013

ISBN 978-1-906613-86-0

Sally Goldsmith hereby asserts her moral right to be identified as the author of this book.

British Library Cataloguing-in-Publication Data.
A catalogue record for this book is available from the British Library.

Typeset by Utter
Printed by printondemand.com
Cover design by Utter
Cover image: 'The Twelve Keys' No. 11 by Tracey Holland
Author photo: ???

Smith/Doorstop Books is a member of Inpress, www.inpressbooks.co.uk. Distributed by Central Books Ltd., 99 Wallis Road, London E9 5LN.

The Poetry Business is an Arts Council National Portfolio Organisation

Contents

9	Hare Ghazal
10	You'll Know Her
11	Received Pronunciation
12	The Bird
13	Lucky
14	Willesden
15	Days of the Commune
16	Heeley
17	Boy
18	Are We There Yet?
19	Winter's End
20	Hand
21	Locket
22	The Robin Clock
23	The Oak and the Fencemaker
24	Fairytale
25	Romania
26	February
27	The Holloway
28	Lil
29	Casualty
30	Beaminster
31	Janice
32	Double Take in Aldeburgh
33	Wind
34	Awake
35	Puppetry for Beginners
36	The Gardening Year
38	Butchers

39	The Mason, Beverley 1349
40	Spitfire
42	The Jubilee Clock
44	Engineer, Dyeworks
45	The Maker
46	Bike
47	Out of Joint
48	Cerebos
49	Beyond the Pale
50	Walberswick
51	Yew And Birds
52	Heeley Retail Park
53	A Walk on the Roughs
54	Eurostar
55	Terns
56	Dipper
57	Pink
58	What the Oak Tree Taught Me
60	Thaw

for Rony and Ewan and in memory of Wanda Goldsmith

Hare Ghazal

*Fleet footed and solitary, makes a shallow scrape or hollow
in clumps of long grass. Does not burrow* for hare

is leaping, zigzagging, doubling back. Somehow it all feels random,
unfocussed, the way you sit at the screen but can't settle. You're hare-

brained, mad as, lolloping from one damn thing to another,
hopping and boxing yourself into this clumsy metaphor.

You think of dusk and the path in a moonscape of dunes,
still your mind, make a noose of it and call her, draw her

*Bawty, Malkin, Scavernick, Skyper, Katie, Laverock,
Caproun, Whiddie, Cuttie, Wintail, Puss* – yes, draw her, *Poor Hare,*

to where you first started her. She held herself in a stitchery of marram,
her glassy eye a window, perhaps a funnel. You pour, hour-

glass yourself back into rank grass, trust that after the running
you will find your form and name: *Old Sally*; your creature: hare.

You'll Know Her

for sure, when she comes at you,
out of her bed of clanking trains,
hooting seas and half-finished nightmares.

You'll know her by the ragbag of scraps and string,
her rabbit paw for luck,
the dead bumble bee in a cough drop tin.

You'll know her by her gripey belly, her bleat,
the stick legs and fluttering hands,
her bones rattling like bikes on roads to factories,

the way she never steps on cracks,
always does what she's told
and says sorry sorry sorry.

You'll know her by the safe place
she keeps her counted knick-knacks,
her cupboard shining with books,

the corners she hides in,
her hoards of pencils and cut up comics,
the pedal car with one pedal and the still spinning top.

You'll know her by her accidents at other girls' parties
and that she might hang out the window,
might smack her brother one with a plastic spade.

Received Pronunciation

As a boy, my Sussex granddad could
spot the runty dillin in a pig's litter,
play the fool down the pleached twittern,
cry fainits when he wanted out of the game,
make jokes about the daglets on a sheep's bum
comparing them to his own number two's.

From the Warwickshire lot I got
the blart of waltzers at Stratford Mop,
learned to swill the sink after washing up,
call down the jutty at the side of the 'us –
loud enough to wake the diddikais about whom
my mother said I never should.

In rural Oxfordshire, I wuz *moi duck*
to aunts who let me tiffle biddy hens
off their eggs, bring in pecked bottles
of *miwk* off of the step, nudged me
out of looking a sawney, warned me
to avoid the bunt of boys or even a cow.

In Sheffield now with you, flower,
I look after us tranklements, crozzle
me bacon and modge me pudding,
put t' door on t' sneck, go to t' foot
of our stairs, let da into t' entry, talk
clarty at neet, laik and love da till ah dee.

The Bird

Off the bus – my aunt – broad face, buck teeth, fat plait,
but exotic in her jiving lilac skirt, stuck out
in a bum ruff of stiff cotton and paper nylon petticoats.

We swing indoors. From her gondola basket, she takes
her tranny and a shoebox pocked with holes. Inside,
the sound of scrabbling. We lift the corner of the lid –

a budgie, day-glo green with black spots,
its horny nose above a toenail beak and claws for feet.
We put it in a cage against the wall in the front room.

There's a mirror, two perches, a sandpaper carpet,
a stalk of millet, a dish, a cuttle fish bone,
and a clown in the corner which bobs up when pecked.

We purse our lips against the wire, make kissing noises,
trot our tongues, sing-song pretty birdie,
hope against hope that one day it will talk.

Each week we let it out for a bit of a flap,
to perch on mum's knitting needles, to scuttle sideways
along the pelmet, to sit on my aunt's shoulder and nuzzle.

When my aunt's nineteen, she marries a man
with Billy Fury hair, has a cake with three tiers
in decreasing sizes. She stays with him, even when.

Lucky

Eight o' clock, relentless steeping rain –
the wheezing bus pulls in a drab grey bay
where water stains the pitted concrete wall
and people shuffle to the parted door.

They're off, we're on, we skitter down the aisle,
swiping hats and hanging off the rails,
hudging up and squealing in the steam
from fug of duffle, soaking gabardine,

we run our fingers round the furry seats,
tease out tickets shoved inside the cracks,
inspect the purple numbers for the magic
sum of twenty one, and smooth them quick,

then into bags and later, out of sight of Miss,
exchange them in dank cloakrooms for a kiss.

Willesden

Sick of the dry cleaning fumes,
I get myself out of the flat
and onto the High Road, past the tube
where it's coming on evening.
A man stumbles out of Ladbroke's –
Postman, Haydock, Ten to one –
then crumples onto the step.

I don't know what to do with myself.
The polystyrene trays outside the Gujerati
chatter in the gutter. It gets later.
It isn't going to get better.

Days of the Commune

High on treeless, pylon planted moors –
two rows of black brick houses, bracken choked,
are slicked with slanting rain.

A lumpy oaten sky sucks at willows by a shed,
the seedy weeds in lines of veg, a sumpy path,
the top of Futters' barn.

Across the swerve of tarmac road, a schoolyard
with its rusting swing, an empty chapel
and a battery farm.

Our terraces – long greasy roofs of lowering slates,
but window frames are bright with yellow, red and blue,
a painted peacock on a door;

the houses arsey versy – yards with privies
by the drive, best faces to the sweep
of peat bog, sedge and carr.

Inside, our queue of scruffs all wait in turn
for thin grey soup, a chunk of heavy bread,
and mugs of Barleycup;

some boilersuited – up for hours of cutting wood
and mucking out – others still in jim-jams –
just got up.

WILL PEOPLE PLEASE NOT ... on a blackboard,
another full of rotas, receipts for stamps, coarse flour,
a pound of two inch screws.

Outside, four nannies tethered roughly on the green
view this world with sly and slotted eyes –
ruminate and chew.

Heeley

Don't know who built this terrace –
some company out to make a fast buck
when the railway came and men were needed
to feed Skeltons' Tools and Hardy Patent Picks.
I don't know who lived here then, when
there were no bathrooms, only tidemarks,
chimneys coughed and you couldn't see
the hills at the end of the street,
when there were no cars parked nose to bumper,
just kids running down jennels into back yards
where they must have tried to grow
a few spuds in earth that hardly saw the sun
and getting caught short in the night
meant a long walk across next door's yard
in the dark; damp newspaper on a nail.
I don't know if the ashes seeded in our garden
came from trees softening this valley
before the railway, the houses, Hardy Patent Picks.
Black bricked corners croak out the names:
Rushdale, Oak Street, Shirebrook Road.

Boy

The night you got picked up by the police,
I slept through it all, no maternal ESP
to locate your scrambled soaked head
that didn't know what you'd done,
and me not knowing what you'd done.

The night you got picked up by the police
a man held a garden fork to your throat
and you said my mum will kill me for this,
but I wouldn't do that baby, I'd never do that.

Are We There Yet?

Here – your hunched back chafes on a trolley
where you snatch each breath, exhale *huh*

another, while two drunks bellow, set off an alarm
and I'm out on the low road, in for the ride, pretending calm

in this hell of a place you're dying in.   *Not long now* –
didn't you say that Mother, in your cherry dress, on our way

to Camber Sands, the suck and draw of waves?
I try to slow, to follow your shallow catch and   *huh*

until day is midnight and you're moved
to M.A.U. I moisten your lips and you mouth   *thank you*

to the nurse who is arranging your head.
Then morning, and loud round the bed, two doctors

too young to be doctors, crowd with their warming machine
and I slip between them and the uneasy chair which in any case

is too far back to see your mouth. Uncertain,
I drag a plastic one which scrapes just this side

of the curtain, across from the wheedling woman
and a raving one who refuses to give her fucking blood.

I look. Your mouth is cracked   *huh*
and I go out for a break. Just a breath of fresh air.

When I come back, it's late. You're already there.

Winter's End

After your last fall we were waiting for it,
that and the brand new wheelchair
and I'd plans to spring you into airy blue –
such larks Mum! Your bent back
would unfurl, a seedling to the laddering sun
and whistling Bing, we'd trundle Shep's Bank
with the zimmer as back up, far
from the fug of your stuffy room
with its prattle of phone-ins and daytime TV
to freshening woods and the trickle of warblers,
a tit's see-saw in the fingers of larches.

Early March, your last and dying day –
how I wished you a soughing breeze to catch
your breath, the tang of sorrel on your tongue,
a stitchwort-starry bank to rest your head
in the fog of the roaring ward. Could you hear
the bleat of fields? Wait now Mother, may I
just lift your top and – *skin a rabbit!* –
lay your bones in clouds of Queen Anne's lace,
wash you soft in froth of cuckoo spit,
then rinse you in this juicy rush of May.

Hand

The bone china got too much to hold, so I took to Mothercare –
    plastic mugs with lids and poky spouts to tip and suck.
        I hid behind the prams and cried. You'd liked your flowery cup.

This old thing! you'd say, spread your shaky fingers on the chair –
    waxy paper skin, knuckles knobbed, but elegant and tapered.
        I'd lay mine next to yours, soothe and cluck, compare our shapes.

A year, but still, these scraps of you. Among my papers there
    you are – the slant that looks a bit like mine: your notes and lists –
        flu jab, frozen meals, chiropodist, – the loops and twists
frayed below the feint lines of the pale blue Basildon Bond:
                      this last unravelled filigree, your hand.

Locket

Death snapped you shut
but I will find your locket,
replace your mum with you,
wear you next to my throat –

not to hutch you, but
to keep you, coax
and kindle you,

my voice there
in its own strained box.

The Robin Clock

All morning the robin has been trying his voice.

I could tempt him with crumbs
then make him a home
in your long brown clock:

late afternoons,
        the spatter
of sad
erratic tickings,

evenings,
his eye in the moon's clicking window,
        he'll peep,
                unwind his thin October song.

The Oak and the Fencemaker

I move up into night until
I'm high enough to catch
the moon and stars and breathe
their silvering, to wind them about
my crown; who can say just what
I might become, head up in the stars.

Not too hard to find you there
in your dark place inside a copse,
to take your burry hide and smooth
the knots that snag my blade,
to tongue-and-groove: nail you tight,
just tight enough to lock all woodlarks out.

Fairytale

Up on the Houndkirk Road
in a foxy coat and pixie hat
with goosey snow deep enough to dream in,
a dripping sun on distant towers sparks
the edge of a corporate world
where the reds might come in the night
and jolly socialist santas bring
new mornings for all the boys and girls,
even the bad girls in their foxy coats
up on the Houndkirk Road.

Romania

Even now, post communism, post Ceausescu
I imagine a patchwork of fields corrugated by oxen,
where bright peasants in aprons stamp their feet
to frantic bouts of fiddling in odd time signatures,
where wooden toys of a sort favoured by the middle class
of Nether Edge are sold at the side of the rutted road
and orphans crowd to the windows of grey institutions
crying out *mămică, mămică*.

February

February cannot remember January –
she is under the frozen earth – and he is
the oldest man, his spine bent wire,
neck bones sprung from a caved chest
and fanning above a mothy collar,
its cloth button hanging by a thread.

He teeters out like a weather-house man
when the glass turns from rain to fair,
pokes in his bag to check his keys,
dot-and-carries down the street to where
the bus might come. He's not afraid
of Death but still can't quite see Spring.

The Holloway

Duck, and you're fed inside
this oak-soaked dark –
a gullet carved from wildwood where
a pheasant's broken clockwork startles.

You're breathed in.
Only rattled blackbirds breach
the arched green hush
where banks are mossed.
Soft earth, hard stone,
leaf-litter, flesh the floor,
and still you are flowed, a boat,
runnelled and cundy borne,
away from heat that frets
in a future – not of your choosing,
yet somehow of your making.

Lil

Young when
eel catching by the sluice,
she'd sensed the green force
come
       minnowing   up   inside
and she knew she'd always have men
easy.

They said she was
loose, a flibberty-gibbet
       or worse,
their eyes watching the wig-wag of her bum
behind her sack apron,
the sinewy legs
       squatting over rows of earthed up tates,
mouth crammed with pork scratchings
from her dockey box.

       Up close –
a breathy *sheela-na-gig*   spread
against the church
wall, breasts like pease puddings,
fenland muck under her nails, raking
the back of each village nit-wit and fancy-pants.

       Even now –
bad breath and lacy teeth – she's a game
old bird, slap-happy and cackling
hipperty-hop from the hedge,
       under a bucking sky.

Casualty

Well Doctor, I was making moussaka for Brian and Pam
and reading *Return of the Native*,

grating the Blue Vinney, relishing
the glare of yellow gorse, its honey smell

sweetening and prickling the simmering sauce.
The big sky of Egdon Heath burned

and Eustacia strode into the kitchen.
I opened the window to let out some steam

and she joined me in slicing plum tomatoes,
staining her hands with the reddle,

smacking her lips over the collapsing flesh
of aubergines. That's how it happened.

Beaminster

In Hardy's Emminster, Angel's church:
swifts scything in blue, tower still
pinnacling to God. Carved high on his perch,

thick legs astride, the flax man flashes
his bag of tools to the stony virgin,
while inside, the parish ladies stitch

themselves into a history thatched
and neat among gentling hills,
their fields sweet with lambs.

In the Square, the chef at the *Wild Garlic,*
will teach foraging, how to tell your fat hen,
from your jack-in-the-hedge, prepare and cook.

Half light, driving home, I peer through
slabs of rain: poor jilted Tess is grubbing roots –
in frozen paws, her sack and chopping hook.

Janice

When you'd gone, I thought of how,
at city's edge, jays flicker out of oaks –
crest-capped and trim on blue electric wings –
and store their seeds in crevices and cracks
against the coming frost. Thus woods
are mothered by forgetfulness of birds.
And when you'd gone, I thought of how,
in each of us, you kernelled kindness
through instances of care you probably forgot.

Double Take in Aldeburgh

You wouldn't be seen dead in there, but I thought
I saw you – huge specs, hoopla earrings, your scrawl
of spiky hair – peering through the distorted glass
of the Cragg Sisters' Teashop, perched like a stroppy owl.
I wish you *were* here, we could scratch our way
to Thorpeness under the gulled and genteel sky,
scorn tidy signs for dressed crab, sole, skate wings.
You'd tell me how pissed off you were to up and die

even though you took your time. Arsier
in death, you thinned yourself to yellow sticks
and I had to dig, get out and past all that. Now there
you are at the café door, larger than life and unapologetic,
clumping out in your agitprop boots, antisocial dog in tow.
Come with me now, let's glare at the sea. Don't go.

Wind

You could try to describe what it does – gusting the road's golden rime
of leaves or scudding plastic bags round a boarded-up precinct;

or you could get down how it sounds: buffeting, racketing,
roaring like a train – you see? You soon descend into cliché.

Wrap up against it then – scarves, woolly gloves, hoods and boots,
cagoules, windcheaters or just toggle up your old duffle,

then look at how some trees nod their heads and curtsey,
how others will sway their arms in a Status Quo, Oasis sort of way.

Or just link and walk – you could get a bit tipsy with its fizz and kick,
like all sense is blown clean out your head and you'll say *I love you*

and not know if you mean it.

Awake

After hours of turning, trying that damn thing
where you count back in sevens,
she putters down to slug vodka, curls
under his coat with the dribbling cat
and yesterday's *Star*, till her mind lifts
up and out with the uncertain birds
and she no longer cares what he said last night.

Puppetry for Beginners

In the attic sorting when I happen upon it,
pull it out and flick through the sections
on *The Puppet's Integrity, Manipulation,
Conveying Emotion Through Gesture.*

Between *Less is More and Find Your Voice,*
I find the letter, the one that said forever,
you'd always love me, sorry for your anger,
and you were seeking help for all that now.

I fold you into a boat, then a paper snapper.
I draw you some tiny teeth with a felt tip pen
give you a pink paperclip to chew. I set you
on the shelf next to *Flaubert's Parrot,*

then I close the book, the last pages,
on *Noh Drama, Ritual, Shadow Play.*

The Gardening Year

All the advice needed for good husbandry is contained in the monthly work sections, © Readers Digest 1969

March: he takes his spade to

> *split old clumps of bergamot and sorrel*
> *sever offsets from Amelanchier Canadensis*

makes sure to

> *water beds with paraquat*
> *spray if aphids or thrips are seen*

She's inside, arranging

> *the beauty of shapely branches*
> *the charm of dried flowers and seed heads*

and dreams of May, June, when he could

> *ease the plants apart with fingers*
> *plant melons in cold frames*

but he is watching for

> *signs of basal rot, fusarium disease, bud blast*
> *controlling the spread of algae by removing with a stick*

July, August: she takes the book to

> *remove blooms as they fade*
> *place orders for new floribundas*

September: she packs it in her case, takes care to

> *save dahlia seed*
> *put sifted bonfire ash in bags to serve as a spring dressing*

October, November: he sets his back to

> *dig borders for winter weathering*
> *make a windbreak of stout polythene*

By December she is settled in Letchworth where

> *planting is possible if the weather is fine*

Butchers

Butchers keep their cleavers sharp,
know a nice piece of topside from a skinny bit of brisket

and ask the women in their shops
if they'd prefer a fat haunch or a scrag end.

They know about chopping, ribbing, boning, filleting,
how to roll tongues and make pork pies with plenty of jelly.

They keep carcasses in walk-in fridges like wardrobes
and ease them off hangers, to order.

They slip little bits of lamb kidney down the backs
of girls' dresses, chase kids up the garden with pigs' trotters.

They garland their front windows with sausages,
garnish their back yards with parsley, never kiss their wives.

The Mason, Beverley 1349

Our master was such a bag of wind himself,
I made his face for the arcading:
pop eyes, fat cheeks, his fleshy mouth
puffing on a blowpipe and filling
the goatskin with his air of self-importance.

I'd nearly finished the job. That night, asleep
among our tools, I dreamed his piper's bag –
filled to bursting, swelling and oozing
in the pit of my good carving arm.
Around, the town droned, humming its pestilence.

Each day brought bodies to the Minster gate –
steeped in a maw of mud among our barrows,
ladders, the pale oolitic stone. I mortared in
my almost finished piper, spotted with the rain,
slunk off through empty streets for home.

Spitfire
for HB

If something was wrong, I'd say so,
not like some

                                      muttering and cuttering.

First off, I was in the Sixth East, ticketing,
where I gave Hetty a piece of my mind
        for sticking the knife

                                      into Olive.
                                      Well! Hetty said, *Just a chip of a girl*
                                      That's it. I've never been spoke to like

Highly delighted I was, I'd told her,
that was what I wanted. I'd told her, oh yes
                that's me,

                                      firebrand all right.

                                      One time Jack Land threatened
                                      to send me to Causer.
                                                          What for
I don't know.
But I said to him, if I go
you're coming as well and I'll tell him
on you and Fred Wright – I know
all about you going into Sixth North
making tea and wasting time –

                                      we'll see about Causer.
                                    So what did Jack say? *Well then Hild*
                                    if you scratch my back, I'll scratch you
                                    Jack Land that was and I had one or
                                    occasions to have bust ups with him

were always trying to get rid of me
  they sent me weighing once
I stuck it about two hours and I said,
there's nobody come near me,
all by myself, there's all this work
ts weighing and I don't know how
hat's it, you can have it,

                      and I was off.

                      Arthur Chamberlain, he wanted
                      to send me to the South Mill

I said, well, I'll leave then
  and I tried for the WAAF

                      but they told me, sorry
                      your work's too important

went to Chamberlain and I said,
can handling cotton be more important
n aeroplanes, how can you say that?
left and went to Rolls Royce

                      to make things for Spitfires.

                      One day an American group came
                      and looked at my work and one said,
                      That's very interesting, what's it for?

I said I haven't a clue.
l, when you do different sorts of screws
this, that and the other, how do you know?

                      I'm sure I don't.

The Jubilee Clock
for JC

Wilf Shardlow's job to keep it to the minute,
see that Belper Town could work to time.
He'd calibrate, adjust, then grease and cosset

Strutt's Mill Clock – the West Tower's crown.
And I, young John, set on apprentice –
not just to oil the frames where lasses wound

the yarn, but to give a hand to wind and fuss
the clock and learn alongside Wilf,
and tweak and tend its apparatus.

Maybe twice a week, I'd steel myself
to follow, climb the Tower stairs up past
the clanking frames, see all the town beneath.

Wilf would take the trap door key, I held fast
my tools and scaled the ladder, ignoring cheek
of girls below, all their flirty banter, till at last –

up, the trap door shut, we'd stop and take
a breather. The winding room – mill muffled –
in there the only sounds the space could make

the steady beat of seconds that calmed our huffing
chests. If the wind was up, we'd almost sway,
two birds, inside its rush and buffeting.

Then we'd nudge and polish, wipe away
the dust, and oil the works, wind the weights –
which effort took our breath from us again.

The chamber where the old clock wore four faces –
each lit by gas and carefully primed –
was even higher, up a wooden staircase

which Wilf and I would slowly climb
to reach the dials. And this was rather odd –
inside the thing, you could not tell the time.

My task: to oil the dials and take care not
to rub the drive shafts, slow its beat –
for all the spinning town depended on this clock.

Once, I forgot to wind, and each I'd meet
would rib me, *Now then, Johnny lad, I see
we're stopped at half past four on every street!*

We tended clock and bell, Old Wilf and me,
and kept the Sewing Company's time some years
until, with buildings left to wind and sky,

the tower and clock were taken down for fear
that they would fall. But we were truly kings
in all those times we'd tend it, gaze out clear

to Derwent, where the mirrored lights would bring
a sense of all that coursing power driving everything.

Engineer, Dyeworks
for SK

He played with Meccano, took the hoover to bits,
but grown, he opened to the ways of the river water,
drew six million gallons from the Amber
still turbid with clay, cleaned it of sticks and muck,
released it, softened, to carry the clarity of dyes –
emeralds, jades, bright carmines, russets,
the many and difficult shades of black.
A spectrometer is safest, no-one sees colour alike...

Later he told her how he found his heart
flickered to see the turquoise flit of a quick bird
among the stipple of ash leaves arching the river,
and once, through the glass of the dye house vats,
gave himself, for the merest of moments,
                    to a welling of blue.

The Maker
for M R Peacocke

No longer the maker and mender of walls,
her hands, she said, missed stone: its pull
and strain on muscles, the tough talk
of fingers, rough edges and lichens.

Bending, she'd sort, trust to her eye,
heft each piece for shape and size
till round its heart stones the wall
stood, a spine curving the hill.

Unsteady on the benty land, she left
the familiar, hard on her freezing fell
and took to town. The maker's knack

to source, weigh, shape flex of line
and turn, she kept. Now face to the wind,
still takes up her words and places, stacks.

Bike

Here I am, pedal-less,
my saddle white
with mould, cogs clogged
with rust and webs.

Give me a break, take me up,
I'd like a spin again,
like in Ardrossan, flying
down to meet the sea.

It's grim in here, the corner
of the cellar, my flabbed tyres
next to a cracked sledge,
a clapped-out mower.

Give me a break, pass me on
to someone with a heart
a tin of 3 in 1,
and a universal spanner.

I'm not any old bike you know,
some sit-up-and-beg;
you'd have liked to see me
in my prime,

derailleurs slick, perfect
rosary click each time
the gradient tipped.
Give me a break.

Out of Joint

Clattering past Bradbury's shop,
Jackie and me
on new Woolworth's skates –
Chuck Berry in our heads
we'd thrust and glide,
thrust and glide,
ker-chunking over flags and kerbs,
the lumpy tarmac where
the garage used to be.

Now, no particular place to go,
down the attic stairs
my creaky feet and ankles clump –
take one step at a time,
one step at a time –
to make my morning cup
and sit and gulp
my calcium pill,
two caplets of glucosamine.

Cerebos

Inside a fusty cupboard, the word
is curled on a blue sky tin
where a boy chases a bird, sprinkles
grains on its tail to catch it and keep,
though he never did. Nor could she,
yet once she believed in a name
like a spell and the magic of salt.

Still, if she unlatches the door
just a crack – sure, it will be dark –
maybe she could reach in, scatter
a handful, strain for the faint notes
of robins in a spinney where
enchanter's nightshade grows,
at the edge of what is there.

Beyond the Pale

There's a longing to be at the core,
the very root of you, to tap
your dark, burrow down, hammer
my bones in the flank of you
and sing inside the resinous funk where
my blood turns in the fork and knot,
hooks up and out into god knows what
in the space outside of who we are.

Walberswick

Dawn, hanging out your socks and somewhere
a skylark sings above the suck of marshes.
The wind shifts, your socks flap to the clap
of a shutter on the bird-legged black sheds,
fastened tight against uncertain water.

Beyond our salty garden, a defensive bank
of grass and shingle, lines of wooden piles
spongy like bad teeth and a swerve of land
where the sea ate a village, its church, spat out
gold sovereigns tied to the shin of a naked man.

The stairs tacked at the back creak like tillers,
as I climb back to you love, our temporary bed
where we're mates for life in our flotsam nest
of old books, reading specs, tea stained cups.
Tomorrow, perhaps, the river ferry and home.

Yew And Birds

> *O, there is a tall tree in the ear!*
> Rilke: *Sonnets to Orpheus*

a tree shaken by Grimm's daughter
                no black pitch   but bright
                          speckles of bird-quaver

a slow rainstick
                tom-tit trickles
                        catching on ear stalks

a mechanical toy from Czechoslovakia
                all whirrings
                        and tintintabulation

a glass celesta
                where a robin in a red pinny dusts
                      her harp of notes

a puppet theatre
                in which wrens cock and flick
                      to and fro on rods

a home for a small feathered soul
                unseen   but busy
                      tapping

Heeley Retail Park

I am wheeling my trolley
past the seed and bones
to a section of *Pets at Home*
hallowed by dim blue light
and shoals of tiny neon tetra.
I could kneel here and pray to fish.

A Walk on the Roughs

It was when I was with Lorna
that I saw him, a stooping man
nudging the corner of my eye,
his eyes hoovering the tussocks.

Autumn's when they do it,
when tiny mushrooms pop up
overnight. As we get close, he says

Hello

trying to appear normal,
not at all like someone
looking for magic.

Eurostar

Now set my mobile back to British time –
that hour now holds me under and I'm lost
to this soft roar that eats imagined rock.
Bright, but out the window formless black,
the only clues the nets for onboard mags,
the underwater mouthing on a neighbour's DVD.

Now the gargling guard in Dutch and French,
but stranger still this travel under tides –
somewhere the swimming ghost of Captain Webb,
the bubbling lips of flickered shoals of fish,
the pops of breath in sacs of bladderwrack.

Terns

They scrap the sky at Howick Scar,
their brains tuned to fish – *kirrick kirrick* –
each rusty syrinx squabbles,
adds to the sea's slap on black dolerite,
the bass loop of this thudding tide.

A faint horizon – stave drawn taut
between the sea and sky – is fixed.
But watch now, quick,

the free jazz scat, as on the fly
they whip and wind then dip below
that line which halves the vastness
to beak and eat, swoop up, spatter
patterns on a page of light,
their skirl of static shredding air.

Dipper

There on a stone,
the bronze melt quick round your feet –
    oh you little switcher swatcher
in your best bib and tucker!

Bessy Ducker,
rock bobber,
intent on the busy brown rush –
    aren't you dizzy
unravelling the braids with your eye?

Tumbler, rollicker,
under-water walker,
finder of grub and fish egg,

then off you zip,
    ripple skimmer –

and oh!
Is that you –
trickled rills and warbles,
all of a gush –
    giving your voice to the river?

Pink

Though there's an ill wind out there
and the chimney's throat gripes
(and it's Autumn, way past berry time),
my heart is about to pink –
perhaps to the salmon of late floribundas
or the delicacy of crabapple jelly.

It is in fact, about to flower, my heart
and may – listen – try its blush of a voice,
a wheezy warble inside its cramped cavity,
then unfurl its rosy bunch of notes
which will seed themselves – puff!
clean out between my ribs.

What the Oak Tree Taught Me
Retreat, 16th October – 12th November 2011

By that time, the blebs in my head
had let in a sky loose with flapping

but then, through the sash's bubble,
I found we were neighbours –
she zigger-zagging her hands
into a crimped green dress,
mine crabbed on the desk.

First, she told me to take a spoon
to my skull, scoop it out,
plug all unnecessary holes,
to be still and not mind the man
with the leaf blower machine.

She said to root down, reach out, drink up,
not to get in a tizz or make a fuss

and we listened together
to the tiny trumpetings of fish in the Esk,
the tinkering of birds –

she showed how to bounce them in my head,
keep them full of flutter and jump.

Sometimes, I made a a bit of a frame
of her to peer through, enter in –
she said you can always find something,
if only a seed or a nut to be going on with.

Other times I watched how her fingers
made a way into a deeper forest,
imagined it there, sucked myself through.
She said to trust the witch, her sweety house.

She sees quite well in the dark of course,
knows how to fizz a bit even when drowsy
and never takes offence at the hooting of owls,

allows others to subtly change her –
lichens, mosses for example – told me
not to mind a slight crust or sponginess in myself.

She says it's good to be wayward,
irregular even, that leaning or drifting
to one side can lead to surprises.

Last, she showed how she softens
into lemony November,
lets leaves drop lightly and settle,
accepting mists and autumn drizzle.

Thaw

A field snapped with frost and stitched with brittle docks,
a metal gate where I hung, still, like the horses there –

the grey standing gentle over the bay mare, held
inside their listening; wick-wick of a pigeon,

the chat of a jackdaw flock. Each second was a frozen bead,
but lovely to the touch. Once, he barely whisked his tail;

I watched. Then shifting my weight against the gate,
both turned and the mare lifted, nut-bright, out of her dream

then came slowly, and again on, slowly; the sky stretched
drum-skin, the sun low and sucked to a thin sweet.

She looked to the grey as if to say, *should I?* and a man
came, walking his dog. The mare whickered. *Grand!*

said the man. *It is,* I said, some strange thing thawing,
and she brought me her breath, timid to my hand.